SANCTITY

SANCTITY

BY

Violet Clifton

NEW YORK
SHEED & WARD INC.
1934

PRINTED IN GREAT BRITAIN
AT THE ALCUIN PRESS, CAMPDEN
GLOUCESTERSHIRE

PROEM

THE life of a Saint cannot be tragedy; therefore what follows is heroic drama.

The sources from the which I have drawn my story are:—

Histoire de Sainte Elizabeth de Hongrie by Charles Forbes René de Montalembert; *Auctor rhythmicus vernaculus de vita s. Elisabethae landgraviae Thuringiae,* auctore Johanne Rothe (Rothe was born in 1360); *Libellus de dictis quatuor ancillarum s. Elisabethae sive examen miraculorum eius; The History of Elizabeth,* by H. A. (1632).

That my thought might be imbued by the period of Lewis and of Elizabeth I read:—*Minnesinger of Germany* by Kroeger; *Poetry of the Troubadours* by Rowbotham; *Troubadours and Courts of Love* by Rowbotham; *Walther von der Vogelweide und die Dichter von Minnesangs Frühling* by Halbach; *Der Singerkriec uf Wartburc;* the accounts of the Courts of Love, by several French authors, as also various accounts of the crusades, including those of Joinville and Villehardouin.

For over twenty years I have contemplated the figure of Elizabeth. As, away from Eastern influences, I moved towards Rome her light guided me. For I thought: "The spirit that fostered hers; that enflamed the wounds of Francis; that gave courage to the wisdom of Katherine; that was meat to the mind of Thomas of Aquinas and of Pascal, and space to the flight of John of the Cross—that spirit sufficient to growth, sufficient to perfection."

When I entered Rome-spiritual Michael and Elizabeth were the names that I added to my names.

I have brooded upon Elizabeth in jungles of Mentawei; in villages of Nias; on coral of Liroeng. In the Island of Islay was written the most of this play.

Test of rhythm—the seven notes of the mating blackcock; test of sweetness—the blossoming magnolias.

I have taken, from the old books, whatsoever I needed; whatsoever I have added is true to the spirit of Elizabeth; I have set all forth in just such words and in just such manner as I felt to be in harmony with this burden.

In the first two versions of this play (of the which I have written four), I gave as the first Scene of Act I the famous contention of poets, and the prophecy of the seer Klingsor, or Elinsor, to which prophecy several references are made throughout the play. This appeared to me to make too long a delay to the immediate action of the play, so I cut it out. The prophecy I gave was according to that in the *Auctor rhythmicus vernaculus de vita s. Elisabethae.*

ELINSOR
I will show you something
new and joyful.
In far Hungaria
now is the dawn.
Aurora, rosy-lipped,
kisses the Sun.
Emergent
from moons of frustration,
Gertrude, Queen of Hungaria,

approaching
to conception.

I hang upon the constellations;
I gaze upon the planets;
I turn about the Ephemerides.
From thighs of Sagittarius,
sign before Capricorn,
I see the sun passing
on toward Aquarius,
the good sign of the outpoured water.
Devoutly I calculate
this shining nativity.

I behold a being
singular in graces
endowed of the Spirit
shining for our joy.
Into Allemania,
into Christendom;
throughout time—
and without twilight.

Let there arise
extraordinary high expectation
of this rare creature
waiting now on threshold of the day,
on the threshold of being.
Singers, knights, Christian people,
great be your joy—
great be your expectation.

CHORUS MYSTICUS

FIR·ST SIDE 🌑 *singing* 🌑

Elinsor well knows
that man is not star-governed
but that according
to God's high-willing
all things, knit together,
affect one another.
Every several body
ministering to its neighbour,
as ordained by law of love.

SECOND SIDE

He beholds the heavens
like to azure pages,
lettered with planets;
therein reading
that which concerns him.
That which to one more artless
meadow-flower would fore-figure,
or bird-migrant flying.
For so—to the shepherds—
little words uttered;
but to the Magi—
truth—wordless,
truth—astral.

BOTH SIDES

The vast obedience of the stars,
their ordered tread, concatenate,
is figure of the harmony
in which this soul, predestinate,
will move to God, as stars to sun.

THE PROLOGUE

CHARACTERS
  THE SEEKING SOUL
  THE CHORUS MYSTICUS

SCENE
  Curtains. A classic figure, to be called THE SEEKING
SOUL, *complains to* THE CHORUS MYSTICUS. THE
SEEKING SOUL, *if so desired, may be retained to watch
the play, seated in a corner.*

NOTE
  CHORUS MYSTICUS. *The author would wish this
band of people to be veiled and robed in wings, and to stand
banked up either side of the stage unseen by the actors, and by
audience seen only when chanting or speaking. The* SEEK-
ING SOUL *does see these figures.*

SEEKING SOUL
Everywhere trace of him I find: everywhere trace;
like footsteps left, or whirr of flying wings
sounding in air.
The acacia, high-set, beckons to the bee;
the jasmine shines, as silver as a star,
so only that the honey-raping fly
may her behold.
The pendant wingèd seeds of sycamore
tend downward to the matrix of the earth—
unto their good they tend,
the flower, the seed:
and I to mine.
But where is gone the spirit of my Lord?
I find his trace ore-seamed throughout the earth,
but that sweet evidence I seek from men
I find not.

CHORUS MYSTICUS
Yet you shall see such holy evidence.

SEEKING SOUL
I sought him by the ocean; I besought:
"O waves, where has he gone that took his way
among your jagged furrows? He that stilled
your tumult with a word and calmed your storms:
I find him not.
O gales that sweep the world, you once lay down
beneath his lifted hand like dragons tamed;
O winds that sweep the world, where is my Love?

CHORUS MYSTICUS
Through all the earth are symbols, hints, and traces
of flaming Love reflected in its works:
the whole concatenation of the sphere
is linked to Spirit. Every creature shows
the Son, the Word, the Image of the Highest,
for every creature is the Maker's art
as Christ the Art of God.

SEEKING SOUL
I stayed a shepherd watching on the flats:
"O shepherd, take me to the Lamb that's slain
for thee, for me!"
I sought the tended flock, enfolded safe:
"O mothering ewes, where is your Shepherd gone
that for the flock would offer up his life?
That youth with pipes
more sweet than pipes of Pan, that Fairest One,
that gentle Shepherd, and that slain Lamb,
where are they gone?"

Amongst the lilies of the field I sought him:
"Where is that Poet gone that praised your day
above the majesty of Solomon?
Make answer, broken reed and smoking flax!"

CHORUS MYSTICUS
Come, see this sign of God, this trace of love;
a silvery trace imprinted in a life,
in span of four and twenty little years.
The virile five-rayed figure of a star,
or form of perfect circle—with return

to point whence it was drawn.

Come, and be glad of courage such as this,
and hear these tidings given of the Most Fair:
as echo, catching up a happy song;
as petal, dear reminder of the rose;
as spring-time, bearing witness that the sun
renews the womb of earth.

ACT I

CHARACTERS

ELIZABETH, *Princess of Hungary.*

LEWIS, *Duke of Thuringia, son of the Duchess Sophia. (He is often called Count Lewis as by affectionate custom.)*

HENRY, *younger brother of Lewis.*

THE DUCHESS SOPHIA OF THURINGIA

AGNES, *her daughter.*

MELCHTIDE, *another daughter.*

GERTA, *a lady-in-waiting.*

AN OLD COURTIER

GENTLEMEN

THE GRAF VON VARILA

THE CHORUS MYSTICUS

SCENE

A great Hall inundated with yellow morning light and with hangings of gold. There is a window looking out to the mountain.

TIME

Morning. Summer, A.D. 1220.

On the rise of the curtain, THE DUCHESS, AGNES, MELCHTIDE, GERTA, *and* A GENTLEMAN *are talking together.* AGNES, MELCHTIDE *and* GERTA *are dressed alike, as is also* ELIZABETH *when she enters. A thread of troubled music is heard just before and during the rise of the curtain.*

AGNES

My lady mother, to-day we were transported to the very zenith of the folly of Elizabeth.

MELCHTIDE

On this, of all days, to have to draw our sleeves before our eyes and to stoop down, hiding our faces.

GENTLEMAN

And that during the most festal Mass of the year. This Assumption of Our Lady, this day of thank-offering for crop and for grape.

AGNES

With the Teutonic Knights inviting our gaze.

MELCHTIDE

And the show of fruit and of grain. The good fruit shining and twinkling but we, unhappy, must cover our faces as though we were penitents, or lepers.

DUCHESS

I had to sign to you to cloak your eyes, and myself did the like, for else we had seemed impious beside the Lady Elizabeth.

GERTA
How, Madam, did this thing come about? I did not
note it for I was busy with my chaplet.

DUCHESS
You, and Elizabeth, Agnes, and Melchtide, with
jewelled gloves, veils, carcanets, and coronets, mantled
finely as I had bidden you be for this feast of the harvest, you, all bright as apple and as corn, knelt near the
great looming cross. Suddenly Princess Elizabeth lifted
her face and shuddered as though asp or wasp had bitten
her.

AGNES
I saw her blush, then grow white, and then fall crump-
led before the cross.

MELCHTIDE
If she never before had seen the image of Christ crucified she could not have been sharper pricked.

DUCHESS
Then she laid aside her coronet and her veil and bent so
low that she swept the stones with her hair.

AGNES
Her head without covering, her hair spilt over the
stones!

DUCHESS
I nipped her: "Demoiselle, straighten yourself. Why
fall like spent horse? Why bend like burdened peasant?
b

Does your crown weigh too heavy?" Elizabeth mur-
mured some excuse, speaking humbly—but again the
cross snatched at her gaze. She weakened, and bowed
down, and wept behind the shelter of her sleeve. Then
it was that I signed to you to draw your sleeves over
your eyes, for to the people we must have appeared
hard-hearted measured against Elizabeth.

She pauses.

In truth, I too saw the form of Christ on cross starkly;
and as for the first time.

*The girls and men whisper and laugh together, all save
GERTA. During the Chant of the Angels, of which they
are unaware as is also the DUCHESS, they occupy themselves in fetching embroidery, preparing a game of chess, and
so forth. The CHORUS MYSTICUS is heard.*

FIRST SIDE
Elizabeth was pricked and pierced by love;
no longer eyes of stone faced carven cross,
illumined eyes gazed on the crucified;
and at the vision her so loving heart
was torn and outraged. This unspoken plaint
we read as from her lips.

*The CHORUS MYSTICUS banked on the other side
of the stage now takes up the words.*

SECOND SIDE
Thou, Jesus, garbed as servant;

I, Elizabeth, thy creature
daring to kneel
decked and haughty;
with carcanets, rings, and coronet.
Jesus despised,
but I, Elizabeth, with equipage
and servers.
How shall I wear this coronet of gold
such wretch as I?
How shall I be adorned
with splendour of a crown
whilst thou, belovèd of my soul, art crowned
with bruising thorns?
I cannot mock thee thus
my tortured Lord.

FIRST SIDE
At that she fell all bent and bowed of shame,
and laid aside her crown,
and pulled her sleeve
before her face, and wept.

AGNES *putting aside her embroidery*
I am surfeited with Elizabeth, for if she games she wins,
ever lucky. Then she claps her hands and dances away
to the poorest of her servants to give them her gains.
When, all night, we are masked and revelling, I have
seen her dance a round or two, laughing and happy,
then stop of a sudden. Once Gerta asked:"Why do you
so stop, Lady?" And the Lady Elizabeth answered:
"One turn," she said, "suffices for the world. The rest
I will forgo for Jesus' sake."

HENRY

I hold her to be mad or bewitched. Woe betide this duchy if ever Lewis marries Elizabeth. She will squander all, and will so indulge the people that they will rise against the nobles.

The girls and men fall to tittering again. One of them gets up and offers the others sweetmeats from a box. ELIZABETH'S *voice is heard, singing behind the curtains at the back of the stage.*

AGNES *looking up*

Here she comes singing, the Lady Elizabeth. Let us bait her.

ELIZABETH comes in, playing with a ball.

GENTLEMAN *kneeling and kissing his hand to her*

Ho, how should one so nun-like play at ball?

SECOND GENTLEMAN

Her play but counterfeits her fortune, for, according to report, this lady's dowry is light as her ball—now in hand, now in air.

MELCHTIDE *laughing*

Truly said—in air since Queen Gertrude, her mother, was murdered, for too often her father in Hungary forgets to send this lady her dowry.

AGNES *angrily to ELIZABETH*

It is well that you have laced your sleeve and now appear as, let us say —a mongolian Princess—instead of joining our company in your favourite guise of servant.

ELIZABETH *troubled*
Lady Agnes, why so angry against me?

AGNES *getting up and coming towards* ELIZABETH
Because in truth I hate you. Long have I hated you, but to-day is the harvest of my complaint.

The others gather round into a group.

MELCHTIDE
This morning you lowered us all.

AGNES
I see you like that white deer that was killed by the herd. *Turning to the gentlemen* Do you remember how the herd pushed it into a shallow pond?

GENTLEMAN
And surrounded it, and butted it back each time it would out, and pushed and trampled it, till the creature died in the water.

AGNES *excitedly, and with gestures*
I clapped my hands and I said: "There drowns Elizabeth, the Tartar!"

The others draw in their breath. Continuing

You are as different from us as the white deer from the

herd and we hate you for that. You have lived in our court for close on ten years and yet you are still a stranger. How shall my brother match with such as you? I tell you this, Lady Elizabeth, that you must change your ways or it is certain that Duke Lewis will not wed you.

HENRY
You should be put into a convent—or a cave.

ELIZABETH shudders and covers her face. GERTA, *who has remained at her embroidery, now throws it down and comes up and puts her arms round* ELIZABETH. *The two girls sadly go out.*

DUCHESS *coming forward*
You did not sweeten your words to her, demoiselle. I see that it is easy to mock at her, and she angers me with her ways all thwart and contrary, unlike what has ever been seen, yet I cannot forget the prophecy of Elinsor. He read in the stars the thoughts of God for this Elizabeth.

She goes towards the window, unconsciously taking up the attitude that Elinsor the seer had taken thirteen years earlier.

We sent ambassadors to Hungary to prove his words, and all was as he had said. The Princess was held to be the good luck of the state of Hungary, the luck-bringer and the bringer of peace. Yes, although Elizabeth be mad and foreign in her ways, I remember that we were

glad of things, strange and rare as herself, that were
sent as gifts from out of her country.

AN OLD COURTIER
For three days the minnesingers—glory of our court
—sang in the far court of Hungary. We had sent them
with the nobles who were to bring the Princess to
Eisenach from Hungary. With thirteen carriages; with
thirteen maidens to bear her company; with horses for
her pleasure; carried in a cradle of silver, and bringing
for her cleansing, bath of silver; clothed all in silk em-
broidered with gold and with silver, so came Princess
Elizabeth to Thuringia. And horses were packed with
presents strange and rare as herself.

AGNES
Apes are rare—spotted bitches strange!

OLD COURTIER
The gifts sent with her were golden vases, sculptured
caskets of ivory, coverings of purple and gold. Never
before had things so precious and so beautiful been seen
in Thuringia.

DUCHESS
Now our workmen make the like, but at that time
such costly goods were new to us.

OLD COURTIER
I see the Princess Elizabeth so: silvery; and a bringer of
treasure.

AGNES

Well, I see her as slut, and as servant; despising things
lawfully belonging to her state, unfit quite as consort
to my brother.

*The sound of a hunting-horn is heard and the calls of
men as to hounds. Beckoning to the courtiers and the girls.*

Come and see if Count Lewis will ride with the hounds
which are to be taken to Green-garth to-day. The
horses are to be tried for their speed. Come, let us watch
their departure.

*They all get up and gradually go out talking and laugh-
ing together. The sound of hunting-horns and cries continues.*
ELIZABETH *comes in sadly, winding wool. She puts down
her yarn and pulls a crucifix out of her bosom and says,
slowly walking, and as though addressing it:*

ELIZABETH

I trust that thou wilt perfect that which thou hast be-
gun. For it is my settled purpose to follow thee as nearly as my state will permit. Thou didst leave heaven:
thou wast poor. If I had many worlds I would leave
them all and become poor as thou. Give me fortitude
to withstand those who would turn me away from that
which I hold to be thy will for me.

THE CHORUS MYSTICUS

FIRST SIDE
O God, stoop to Elizabeth

and over-wing her!

SECOND SIDE
May she not be as doll nor as puppet;
nor as shuttlecock batted in play;
nor as kite before the wind.

FIRST SIDE
Watch that she be not the toy of accident
like to those who do not stay their doings
in the shelter of thy wings.
For they are but the playthings of the lesser earthly law.

SECOND SIDE
Allow not the mindless winds of chance to blow upon
    Elizabeth.
But let her feet stand planted in thy heart,
for she is thy crop and thy creature;
she has interwoven her will with thy most holy will.

*ELIZABETH has taken up her bobbin again, and she
walks about, musing. The* GRAF VON VARILA *comes
in.*

VARILA
Why so heavy of heart, Lady?
Have you not seen the Landgraf
since his return?

ELIZABETH
I have not seen Count Lewis.—
The Lady Agnes told me

I am unfit to be his bride.
Not true to my estate
but like a servant.
I wonder
if Lewis sees me so.
He was ever wont to bring me
on his return
a toy from somewhere;
gloves cunningly broidered
or a little knife.
The gifts no matter;
they were tokens
that he had thought of me
in the market-place
or city:
"These jewels
like to thine eyes," he said.
A coral pater-noster
once he gave me:
"For coral lips that pray."
Yet this return
was like a day of winter
without a gift.
All have marked the lack.
The courtiers mock me.
Lewis's empty hands are of no matter
so long they be not
a symbol of his heart voided of me.
All other times I ran to make my curtsey,
and then he gathered me
into his arms
caressed and fondled me.

I gave him share of my most secret thought,
he never chided,
he found no fault
in that I love the simpler sort of people
the shepherds and the children;
he only laughed in gentleness, and called me
his sister from afar;
his foreign maid;
his playmate from a country quite remote.
I would I knew if Lewis loves me.

VARILA
I think, my Lady, that Count Lewis loves you,
but he has cares that bolt his mind
against the gentler things.
I do not doubt his mind is set towards you.
But see, he comes.

❧ VARILA *looks out of the window as though towards
Lewis.* ELIZABETH *slips her hand into that of* VARILA. ❧

ELIZABETH
Plead for me, dear Count, you who are as a father to me.

❧ *She goes out.* LEWIS *comes in with his hound and an*
ATTENDANT, *but he signs to the attendant to leave him
alone with* VARILA. *Exit the attendant.* LEWIS *greets*
VARILA. ❧

LEWIS
Grand Master of the Hunt, what is the outcome of my
new laws? Yourself was in doubt as to their wisdom.

VARILA
Indeed, Sir, when you gave weapons to the peasants wherewith to protect their crops from stag and boar, I feared that they would hunt the game and drive it far into the forest.

LEWIS
The peasants are busied dragging from the earth their meagre living. They will but drive off the creatures that near their corn. Beyond that they will not harm our hunting.

VARILA *surprised and with admiration*
Sir, that in truth is what is done, and the small people work with hearts refreshed, knowing that what is planted will be reaped.

LEWIS
Very grievous was the sound of the rattles ringing and clapping all the night. Toiling by day, the peasants yet had to watch by night, on guard against the wild beasts. And the dreadful forfeit, though never I saw that exacted, the loss of his left hand if a man raise weapon against marauding boar or stag! Now that this thing is bettered, I feel at peace.

VARILA
Sir, may I speak to you bluntly, as an old man?

LEWIS
Speak, I will answer plainly.

VARILA
Sir, what is your intent towards the Lady Elizabeth?
She, that nine years ago I brought to you, cradled in
silver? I laid her beside you on the ancestral bed. She
was but four years old; you were eleven. Would you
be freed of the word given on your behalf to the King
of Hungary by the Duke your father? Would you now
wish to send the Princess back into Hungary?

*LEWIS goes to the window, then, returning, takes VON
VARILA by the arm, leads him to the window, and points
to a height rising out of the plain.*

LEWIS
Look now at Inselberg
reared from the plain
sky-high, in throng of cloud!
Were Lucifer
to swear that from the base
to very crown
the hill should be a height of gold,
the sum of it a-top, a-down,
mine to possess
so only I forswore Elizabeth,
I'd scoff at Lucifer.

Pause

Were Inselberg all rough with ruby stones,
with chrysoprase for rock,
diamonds for dew,
and pearls for pebbles,

and all that treasure mine so I forswore
my betrothèd sister, sweet Elizabeth,
I'd answer Lucifer: "I love her more
than all my territories, all my towns,
than fame or name, than battles, laurels, crowns,
her worth beyond the worth
of mountain turned to ore.
She is my pulse, my goal,
far dream, and secret core."

Nine of my nineteen years have bound to me
my betrothèd sister, sweet Elizabeth.
And nine times since she came
in silver cradle,
silvered from Hungary,
spring's golden flame
has lit our love again.
Tendril of travellers' joy,
tether of woodbine,
nine times have bound us nearer.
Garlands of violets and anemone,
fetters of flowers, and cowslip chains,
made her the dearer.
From out the nests
nine times have gone
the minnesingers of the spring,
nurtured by feathered breasts that shook with song,
nurtured by flying wing.
The music, all the sap and scent of May,
the honey-trove, the strength, the quick-life surgent,
the promise of the spring, and all the urgent
deep-natured mysteries of the fostering earth—

all woven in with sweet Elizabeth.

The stage is blotted out and only the CHORUS MYST-ICUS *is lighted.*

THE CHORUS MYSTICUS

FIRST SIDE
So was God's wish for man
in paradise
in Eden.
There as here
two lovers from the hand and breath of God.
A man, a woman
perfect dual thing;
five-petalled star;
from holy wish, from God-thought brought to be.

SECOND SIDE
For seven years
these star-like, star-told lovers
will tread their sun-path.
Hand in hand
heart in heart
side by side
soul-soaring.
Then one of them
for Christ's renown must die;
and one of them
for Christ's renown must live
until her circle be completed
and her course

ended in God.

FIRST SIDE
Eia glad lovers! loving with the flesh.

SECOND SIDE
Eia espousèd in the spirit part!

BOTH SIDES
Hail sacramental lovers! grace transcended.

ACT II
FIRST SCENE

CHARACTERS

ELIZABETH, *Princess of Hungary, Duchess of Thuringia.*

LEWIS, *Duke of Thuringia, her husband.*

HENRY, *younger brother of Lewis.*

MASTER CONRAD, *confessor to Elizabeth.*

YSENTRUDE, GERTA, *ladies-in-waiting to Elizabeth.*

WALTHER VON DER VOGELWEIDE, *poet.*

THE EMPEROR FREDERICK

RUDOLPH VON VARILA, *son of the Graf of Act I.*

MONK ROBERT

A FRIAR OF FRANCIS, *formerly Confessor to Elizabeth.*

TWO CRUSADERS

AN OLD COURTIER

THREE COURTIERS

TWO KNIGHTS

THE CHORUS MYSTICUS

SCENE

One long room, curtained with red, purple, gold, and sapphire, as deep and brilliant as possible, leaving curtained off on the right a small closet, in which ELIZABETH *will be seen alone with her husband. This is curtained in white, so that the closet may have a cell-like appearance. At the opening of the scene only the closet is seen.*

TIME

Nearly seven years later.

C

ELIZABETH is sitting and spinning, half-singing to herself.

ELIZABETH

How I delight in handling this coarse wool, spinning, carding, or winding on the wheel what others have spun. How gay to carry hanks of yarn to be woven to cloth and given to the Friars. Yet my so doing scandalises the ladies of the court, and therefore, ah-la-la, ah-la-la, I hide myself to do the work that pleases me.

LEWIS comes in excitedly. She runs to him and they embrace.

LEWIS

Sweet sister, hast heard the news?

ELIZABETH

What news, I pray, dear brother?

LEWIS

Near at hand is the Emperor Frederick. I met him as I hunted, by a chance only—for he was travelling fast so that his passage might not be marked. When he knew who I was he said sudden: "I will return to Wartburg with you so only you entertain me as I ask." "Sire, in what manner may that be?" I asked. "Meat, wines, music, and my loyalty I can offer. Is there something more that I can give?"

ELIZABETH

What answer did the Emperor make?

LEWIS
He said: "I ask to be a little while with your chief and greatest good. I would see and I would talk with the Princess Elizabeth of Hungary."

ELIZABETH *surprised*
My sweet love, let the Emperor be heartily welcomed.

LEWIS
As I hurried towards thee I called to Gerta and to Ysentrude, bidding them find festal garments for thee. They answered that thou art but ill-furnished with ornament and apparel, having but lately bestowed all upon the poor.

ELIZABETH *laughing*
I will be so gay and so welcoming that the Emperor will not mark my lack of gold ornament nor of velvet mantle. I shall please him as though I rustled in silk.

LEWIS *with grave agitation*
Yet, indeed, I would thou couldst receive the Emperor according to our estate. Ah! would there were time to furnish thee anew. I desire it for mine honour's sake. I would not wear the ugly appearance of slighting thee —as though I did not love and honour thee. Alas! thou wilt appear as one uncherished.

ELIZABETH
Ah, sweet friend, thou dost shun the very appearance of evil. Wilt thou not say I am in bed? I will gladly go.

LEWIS
That I cannot do. I made promise to the Emperor.
Dear glutton of God, sometimes I could wish that thy
hunger after righteousness were not so sharp—for it
brings me suffering.

He sighs.

ELIZABETH *nearly crying*
My gentle, my beautiful, my Lord,
I will do thy desire.
Indeed I will do thy bidding.
I shall not fail thee.
I shall appear all glorious to the Emperor.

Pause

The ruby stone of charity is bright,
azure of prayer
and sumptuous purple of a mantling love;
I will pray these be made visible and outward.
My beautiful, my gentle, my liege Lewis.
God willing, I shall seem magnificent,
and that because of thy desire.
I will not thwart thee
who are built up in goodness.
Henceforward I will do all thy will,
for after God thou art my lord.

LEWIS
But, sweet sister, how wilt thou compass this?

ELIZABETH *gravely*
Go away for a little. I will follow. Have no care for my apparel, for I believe that our Lord will provide for our honour.

LEWIS goes out. ELIZABETH *puts on an old cloak, saying as she does so,*

ELIZABETH
I will pray mantled so, for thus I do whenever I would storm heaven.

Pausing as she draws the cloak round her

Dear tattered-often, often-mended mantle of Francis, friar of Assisi, dear tattered mantle sent from one lover of poverty to another such lover.

She kneels down and prays fervently.

Mercy of Christ, encompass me,
glory of Christ, encircle me,
I am bereft, ungarmented and bare,
despoiled for love of thee.
Clothe me, bejewel me, shine all about me.
Be marvellous to me.
Make seen, for just a little time,
the unseen glory that I wear within me.
I have given thee much, be not behind-hand in giving.

Darkness blots out the closet. The CHORUS MYSTI-CUS *is heard.*

FIRST SIDE
For a brief time
may men see her
as we see her,
shining.

SECOND SIDE
Our power be upon them
that they may behold
the inward glory
made manifest.

The Hall is now disclosed, with LEWIS, CONRAD, YSENTRUDE, GERTA, VOGELWEIDE *and other* GENTLEMEN.

LEWIS *to the Company*
My lady will not delay her coming.

VOGELWEIDE *to* GERTA
Oh, indeed, I desire to see your lady. I was at Eisenach when Elinsor foretold her. Can it be that she is even as he forehoped?

GERTA
Even the shining of the stars could not express her beauty. She is of the pleiades of the saints. I am so happy day by day seeing her, that I lift up my mind often to say: "Thank God for her; thank God for Elizabeth."

The EMPEROR *enters.* LEWIS *goes towards him, and all the others advance to meet him.*

LEWIS
Sire, you are rested and refreshed?

EMPEROR
That I am. And I have seen here what I never thought
to see, a court wherein is no blasphemy. Elsewhere the
chief evidence of men's faith is in the oaths with which
they stress their sayings. I am told also that there is no
light traffic with carnal love. Yet the court is gay
enough and pleases me.

VOGELWEIDE
The court as it was in the time of Duke Hermann will
be conserved to the ages, kept ever in our songs.

OLD COURTIER
Some of your songs, Sir, gave an itch to the Duchess
Gertrude and to the Duke, though they pleasantly
tickled the rest.

VOGELWEIDE ✿*to* LEWIS✿
These, Sir, you must forgive. I praised your father, but
it was my way to laugh at this—at that—at my own
poverty and at the Duke's munificence.

✿*Laughing*✿

I used to make him frown by my impudent greeting:
"Good-morrow to both bad and good." But, indeed,
all kind were here assembled. The Duke Hermann ex-
celled in the gai-savoir.

LEWIS ✿*to* VOLGEWEIDE✿
You sang once that you never yet enjoyed more than
half a day of happiness.

VOGELWEIDE
Maybe a poet asks too much of the hour. It was dreari-
ness to look back on long years of fighting. I complain-
ed of our over-much fighting; and my poverty was
irksome. But now the Emperor has given me a fief. I
have a dwelling and land of my own, and now I sing:
>   Listen, every man! I have a fief!
>   I have a fief!
My last poem is a lament for much that I see passing all
too quickly away. Yet in this last poem I look forward
in hope—for with the Emperor I am to fight for the
freeing of the Holy Land. I never yet saw the Holy
Land. Shall I sing you the last part of my song?

LEWIS
Yes indeed, do so.

VOGELWEIDE ✿*singing or reciting*✿
Evermore I should sing: "All's well!"
And never more "Ah me!"
Could I but gain Jerusalem
past plain, hill, plough, and sea.
For so, poor serf, or richest lord,
with shield and consecrated sword
can gain from Christ a crown to have in heaven,
all God's long-time; untouched by morn or even.
Evermore I should sing: "All's well!"
And nevermore "Ah me!"

If, joyful to Jerusalem,
crusading forth fared we.
Evermore: "All's well, all's well!"
And nevermore: "Ah me!"

EMPEROR
Ah yes, the crusade, the crusade!

❧Repeating❧
I evermore should sing: "All's well!"
Nevermore: "Ah me!"
Nevermore: "Ah me!"
I am about to fulfil my long promise to the Pope and
shall go to Jerusalem—in a dream I foresaw myself
wearing the crown of Jerusalem and for Christ's honour I would that I might wear that which for Christ's
honouring Godfrey of Bouillon refused. After two
hundred years of fighting the time must be ripe for a
christian ruler to hold that crown.

MASTER CONRAD
I, Sir, have been preaching this crusade in Allemania,
for it seems that the call has come to Allemania.

EMPEROR
Landgraf, will you not accompany me with a host?

LEWIS *❧gasping❧*
Sire—Sire—

EMPEROR
Why do you hesitate?

LEWIS
Sire, for two reasons. The first that I have reforms in hand. I am mending the laws of my nobles as towards the fiefs and the peasants, and this is a hard task and long, for I would not cause undue irk to my nobles, yet there are usages that should be righted. The second reason is that my Lady is again fruitful and I can scarce find it in my heart to leave her.

EMPEROR *sarcastically*
Ladies bear well with such separation. You be behind the times here in Thuringia. Some forty years ago in France the Comtesse de Compagne and her Court of Love agreed and affirmed that love cannot exercise its power on married people.

MONK ROBERT
Sire, forgive me if I cry folly to that ruling of the Court of Love. Our Duke and his Lady love each other beyond what can be believed and they seek every occasion of being together. They should not be separated.

MASTER CONRAD *aside*
Yet—for the building up of her soul—such parting might profit Elizabeth.

A COURTIER *aside*
The Duke excuses his lack of zeal for wounds by his zeal for his lady.

HENRY *to himself*
My mother holds Elizabeth to be a witch; and Lewis shows himself bewitched.

A FRIAR
The Duke is doing great things in this land of Thuringia. He alone, of all rulers, never gives benefice to priest because such a priest is rich or learned. Every priest must follow the gospel and must be above the evils of the time; and this is Master Conrad's teaching.

MASTER CONRAD
Sire, I never temper my words, and I have told the Duke that it is more evil to put into power a wicked priest than to kill a hundred men. For greedy priest blights the purses of the people and destroys their souls by withholding the sacraments for his own ends and by impairing the belief of the faithful. Such priests make null the death of Christ. They make it null, void, and unavailing.

MONK ROBERT
The Spirit of Christ is blowing through Thuringia, and Christ has left his tomb. The tomb is empty. Why seek him there? Why take up sword to kill rather than pursue the merciful works of his Spirit?

All look shocked; they whisper and shrug their shoulders.

MONK ROBERT
Forgive me if I scandalise you, I may be in error.

A CRUSADER stands forward.

CRUSADER *angrily*
They who take the sword perish by the sword; many of

us gladly so have perished, that is, their bodies were slain.
But I hold that our souls do gain thereby. Jerusalem for
christians—that is a point of honour. It can scarce be
reasoned about. It is apprehended here *pointing to his
heart.*

SECOND CRUSADER
In a parable I will make clear this honour. Were lady,
beloved of knight, to be dead and laid upon her bier, it
were unreasonable and useless to defend her body
from sacrilegious hands stretched out to do her dishon-
our—for being dead she were insensible of shame. Yet
any one of us would die to save such untenanted flesh
from desecration. And so is the love we have to the
tomb and to the Holy Land of Christ and Mary.

A THIRD CRUSADER *taking up the argument*
I hold that where Christ trod there christians must be
free to worship. The places where suffered the holy
must be surrounded by lovers, and not by infidels.
These paynims, to a man, would die to keep us from
Mecca, so Saracen ruler himself told me. Do we not
love the tomb of God as well as they love the Mecca of
their prophet?

EMPEROR *to* LEWIS
Ponder the matter and join me if you be able.

*LEWIS covers his face for a few seconds, thinking. Then
he goes up to the* EMPEROR.
LEWIS
The knights' words stung me as touching my honour,

and, above all, the honour of Christ. Sir, give me the cross but *turning to all* I shall not as yet wear it openly nor none of you must reveal this matter, for I shall wait my time. But I swear that I will go to Jerusalem.

The EMPEROR *gives* LEWIS *a crusader's cross, which he receives kneeling.* LEWIS *puts the cross into his wallet.* VOGELWEIDE *sings again the last verse of his lament. Just as* VOGELWEIDE'S *song finishes* ELIZABETH *enters. She is in purple, with an azure cloak, pearls, rubies, topaz, sapphires, and perhaps turquoise. Very gorgeous. The* COMPANY *gasps and stands up. There is a buzz of exclamation.*

A COURTIER *aside*
She is more gorgeous than the Queen of France.

HENRY *sneering*
She goes ever to excess, dressed as widow when her lord is absent, now she is clothed like a goddess. The peacocks of Juno in their pride would be drab beside her.

A THIRD
We never before saw her so displayed.

HENRY
Wasteful always—if not on the poor then on herself.

The EMPEROR *nears* ELIZABETH *and they bow to each other. He leads her to a chair where he can see her.*

L E W I S *stands by her chair. The others stand and move about.*

EMPEROR

Lady of Thuringia, Lady of Hungaria, I have long desired to see you, for Walther von der Vogelweide has told me of the prophecy of Elinsor; of a great expectation, and of a light shining.

ELIZABETH *looks embarrassed.*

ELIZABETH

Walther von der Vogelweide was of those who brought me here to Thuringia when I was a child.

EMPEROR

I see now fulfilment of that starry prophecy.

ELIZABETH

The prophecy, Sire, is still far from its fulfilment. When I think on it—and that is seldom—I tremble, for alas, I often offer obstacle to grace, although I have great occasion for virtue.

EMPEROR

There are things I would ask you and things that I would tell you, Lady Elizabeth, and in me I pray you see not to-night the Emperor of the Holy Empire, but instead, a poet resting in your castle.

L E W I S *fetches a goblet of wine and gives it to the* EMPEROR.

EMPEROR *to* LEWIS
Tell me, Duke of Thuringia, of the great famine of last
year, and of how your lady contended against it. For I
heard many tales, each one contrary to the other.

LEWIS
I was far off when the crop failed. I was visiting my
people on the farthest marches of my dominion.

RUDOLPH VON VARILA
A little blue blight on the leaves and on the stalks of the
growing things: "What is it?" we said, "that, like the
wings of a butterfly, has touched the fields?" "How
pretty! How pretty!" the children cried. And two days
later all was black, rotted, and wilted.

A MONK
Soon the people ate carrion. O Christ, what dreadful
things we saw done.

A KNIGHT
The Lady Elizaeth prayed. Then she flung open the
granaries and every day, orderly, she fed the poor.

FRIAR OF FRANCIS
She fed them but, too, she gave them seed to plant. She
saw to it that they laboured so that the next year come
not so dreadful.

HENRY
We all cried out to her to stay her hand.

LEWIS ❧*sternly*❧
They called my wife prodigal. They called her waster of my estate. When I returned from Apulia the court-iers, and the stewards and wardens of my estate came towards me on the road to make complaint.

❧ELIZABETH *laughs.*❧

ELIZABETH
My dear brother said only: "O let my lady be. It is well that she should send booty before us into Paradise."

MONK ROBERT
How, indeed, should she send the hungry away, for she and Duke Lewis see in the poor the ambassadors of God?

LEWIS
I said to the courtiers and to the stewards: "All is well so only she leave me Wartburg and Naumburg. Of the rest she may dispose."

MONK ROBERT
As it happened, the crop sown in thankfulness by those the Lady Elizabeth had saved was so abundant and so rich that the great drain laid on the Duke's riches was soon made good to him.

EMPEROR
I heard many tales—one of loaves of bread turned to crimson roses.

ELIZABETH laughs and, getting up, she takes the goblet from the EMPEROR and gives it to a PAGE, thus cutting short the EMPEROR'S story.

ELIZABETH *turning to the EMPEROR*
Sire, I am not lettered. Tell me something of this era of the which you are the pinnacle.

EMPEROR *after thinking for a moment*
I hold that we of this age will be remembered for the two loves that light us: First is our love for the tomb of Christ; the dumb lips of a thousand thousand dead speak best of that; and, after that, is our festal love of women. The knight with his sword, the poet with his song, and the countryman with his hundred flowers named after her, each, following his fashion, acclaims Mary. Our minnesingers sing Mary; the spring season; and the loveliness of women; threefold glory of our earth. Lady, I see in you the perfect blossom of the poet's expectation; the flowering of the seer's starry hope: rock-rose of Allemania, sweet sun-dependent flower.

A KNIGHT steps forward.

KNIGHT
Sire, may I speak and tell you of the manner in which this lady has brought me fortune? She stands apart and stores all her glances and all her sunshine for Lord Lewis and for the poor of God. Yet from her I have got a jewelled glove. See, I wear it on my casque. For past six years I have been knight invincible in the fight, yet before that I was timorous and feeble.
d

ELIZABETH *interrupting*
I never gave such a favour to any man.

KNIGHT
Lady, you gave it to a poor unfortunate. At first you
said: "I have no money with me." But he urged in
Jesus' name that he could not wait so great was his
need. He urged with the Holy Name, and your colour
came and went. From off your hand you pulled a
jewelled glove, then ran quickly for Duke Lewis
awaited your coming. I paid the man an honourable
sum, and I bought this happy treasure.

EMPEROR
Tell me, Lady, how comes it that you, who so often,
it is said, go hungry—for in spite of your gay devices
that has been marked—how comes it that you set such
store on feeding the hungry?

ELIZABETH
Because, Sire, that hungry mouths cannot praise God.

EMPEROR
Why do you wash and tend them? Why cannot another do this on your behalf?

ELIZABETH
Sire, we wait willingly on those we love, nor do we call
to a servant, "Hie, bring this cordial to my child." But,
with our own hands we minister. Even so do the
Knights Hospitallier on the fields of battle.

EMPEROR
Granted, but how comes it that the wretched are so dear to you?

ELIZABETH
In every sufferer I see the sufferings of Christ. Then again I see the stricken as having power to exercise patience and I say to them: "Let not your sufferings be barren as winter stick. Instead, make it flower into patience so that you have a rare offering for God." That they should suffer in body and not, by alchemy of spirit transform the suffering to merit, that, Sire, were grievous miss.

EMPEROR
Yet another question, loveliest of ladies. Tell me, what is your heart's wish for every man? Is it that all men should have wealth, or that all may have a blessed poverty, since you, like Francis the Friar, are enamoured of poverty? What, indeed, *is* it that you desire for each one of your subjects?

ELIZABETH *laughs and claps her hands.*

ELIZABETH
O Sire, I have but one wish and a simple one, and never I give bread or money but that I whisper my wish to my angel. Never do I wash wound, nor bind up break, nor kiss running sore, but I say inwardly: "Sufferer, may you see God, may you see God, may you see God!"

EMPEROR *touched*
The Duke Lewis gave me entertainment and meat and

drink, and you, Lady, have given me another wine as from a sunny slope; honey as from a flowering hill. I am poet as well as warrior and emperor. I am christian too, though I often rail against pope and priest. But it is to the poet in me that you have spoken—and I thank you, Princess Elizabeth.

ELIZABETH rises. The Company all move. The EMPEROR kisses ELIZABETH's hand and they take leave of one another. The stage is blotted out and, when the lights go up again, ELIZABETH is shown, plainly dressed and back in the white closet. Perhaps music here. After a slight pause, LEWIS comes in.

LEWIS
How, Elizabeth, didst thou of a sudden become so glorious? From whence thy jewels and thy dress?

ELIZABETH
Did I not tell thee that I serve One who has care for thine honour and for mine? I prayed and he heard me.

LEWIS
Truly, it is a good God that we love. There is joy in the service of so good a master, that faithfully comes to the help of his own. May I, from henceforth, be more and more his servant.

The stage is darkened. The CHORUS MYSTICUS is heard.

CHORUS MYSTICUS

FIRST SIDE

Miracle—Miracle!
Elizabeth had need; her love the cause
of that sharp need, so Love made good her want.

God does not overturn his natural laws,
but eagle-sweeping faith can over-slant,
and soaring, planing prayer can over-wing
ten thousand lesser laws.

SECOND SIDE

That none may hold
this miracle a breach of law, we sing:
"God never breaks his law: lit flax shall burn,
but rain may slay the fire, extinguishing
the leaping flame. Remedial plant can turn
the flow of poison in a sick man's blood.
And all can be attained by those that learn
in trust to fling themselves upon the flood
of love and prayer, which powers over-ride
the lesser powers and laws, and quite out-stride
but never countercharge the ordered tide
of consequence:
of God-made consequence, and God-made law."

ACT II

SECOND SCENE

CHARACTERS
- ELIZABETH
- LEWIS
- YSENTRUDE
- GERTA
- THE DUCHESS SOPHIA
- THE CHORUS MYSTICUS

SCENE

A big bedroom with the ancestral bed, lacquer-red draperies, but this room is not shown at the beginning of the scene.

Instead, is shown a closet, off the bedroom, as in the previous scene. This may be white and cell-like, or may be red.

TIME

A few months later.

⚘ *On the rise of the Curtain,* Y S E N T R U D E *is dressing* E L I Z A B E T H's *hair.* G E R T A, *minstrel-like, is singing a little mocking song.* ⚘

GERTA

But yesternight,
lady she sighed:
"I would I were
the Lord Christ's bride."
But yesternight
lady she said:
"Would that Christ owned
of my girlhood
its greatest good."
Lord Lewis draws nigh,
lady weeps no more,
gay as blue sky,
heart light as song,
light as may-fly.
Because heart's core
lord Lewis draws nigh.

But yesternight
lady she dressed
as claustral widow
or anchoress.
But yesternight
lady, she said:
"For love of God
leave to the sea
the pearls that be.
Leave fur to wolf,

leave gold to earth
deep in her bowel.
We to our prayers,
leave feather to fowl;
our pomp, our mirth,
be in the soul."

ELIZABETH *gravely*
True, Gerta, I said, Leave entrailed in the earth its gold,
and leave in the belly of the sea the pearls of shells. Be
clothed, instead, in simpleness, for I see us daughters of
God, so lustrous that all outward glory is but shadow of
our inward shining. Whenever my husband returns,
then it is good that I should meet him dressed as befits
his Princess and that in his eyes I should be pleasant and
gay for our love's sake. Indeed, he might otherwise be
tempted to sin. I did weep my forfeited virginity when
I considered how precious is virginity. I grieved because I had withheld a gift which I might have dedicated
to God. Yet I believe that my present state is God's
will for me. Deck me, therefore, and garnish me, for
Lewis loves me and would see me lovely—as are all the
works of God's power. Lewis is the ocean of my con-
tent. I would embrace him with the kisses of a hundred
mouths, even as the Nile, with a hundred mouths,
flows out upon the sea.

YSENTRUDE
Lady does well to deck her, for the courtiers cannot
cease from trying to beguile Count Lewis, although
each time he rebukes and sharply punishes.

GERTA

I was told that on his last journey, having stayed at the house of his kinsman, supper and entertainment being ended, the Count withdrew. He commended himself to God and to his angel, and slept. A woman, rampant of lust or greedy for gold, stripped herself, got into his bed, and lay at his side.

She stops as ELIZABETH *utters an exclamation.*

Disturbed by the rustle of her silks, or wakened by his good angel, the Count sprang out of bed and calling to his gentleman—Rudolph von Varila—he told him to lead the woman away.

YSENTRUDE

But, being Knight of great courtesy, Count Lewis said: "Give her gold from my purse, for only the sore need of it could have brought her to this pass."

GERTA

Varila asked: "Sire, are you not tempted?" And the Count said: "Even if I did not detest the sin of adultery, yet I would not do so great an injury to Elizabeth, for she is my beloved wife."

ELIZABETH *falls on her knees.*

ELIZABETH

O God, thou hast preserved our union here, give us the union of the life eternal.

They hear steps and voices in the big bedroom through the looped curtains. ELIZABETH springs up.

I hear my husband's voice.

ELIZABETH and her ladies pause before going through the curtains and they hear the DUCHESS SOPHIE speaking.

DUCHESS
Elizabeth blasphemes; she is evil. In the orchard yester-day, there where she counted on the shelter of the apple-trees, I heard her, and through the leaves I saw her. She sat on a log, and at her knee knelt a scurvy fellow, he one of those wretches so crowned and shod with disease that not another would touch him. Elizabeth put unguents on his head and she combed his hair, matted with sores, as though she handled fine silk. And she crooned to him: "I see in you the likeness of my God: God's image and his superscription here." I clapped my hands to my ears for fear of such profana-tion. I thought God would strike her. I am daunted yet by her "Image of God."
Can no stench stay her? Does she dote on sores? Has she no likeness to us, her kindred? She so far outlandish that she appears as a strange creature, half-monster, half-woman. Our merriment leaves her sedate. Instead, she pleases herself—daring disease and squandering on the poor.

The DUCHESS takes LEWIS'S hand and pulls him to-wards the bed.

Come, see now what your Elizabeth has done. She who honours no custom cares not even for the bed of your ancestors, the bed on which your pretty babes were begotten and born. See how she loves another more than you, see how she has befouled your bed. *She draws the curtains of the bed but is distracted by the sound of* ELIZABETH *coming in from the closet. She looks away from the bed towards* ELIZABETH *while she finishes speaking to* LEWIS. ... In your bed—a leper!

LEWIS gazes at the figure on the bed which, however, must be obscure to the audience. The DUCHESS *is still turned towards the closet, through which* ELIZABETH *has come that she may soften the expected anger of her husband.* LEWIS, *having looked with great intensity and emotion at the leper, quickly draws to the bed curtains.*

ELIZABETH
My liege, I hid him here not knowing where to lay him ... poor Helias, the leper.

LEWIS
Sweet sister, to such guest our mutual bed be welcome ... *pausing, then speaking to* ELIZABETH *alone.* ... for it was not Helias that I saw before me but— stretched upon our bed—Christ as the Crucified. *He falls on one knee and speaks as though to himself, deeply moved.* I am all unworthy to see such a marvel as I have seen, to hold such treasure as I do hold.

YSENTRUDE has by this time advanced into the bed-chamber.

To YSENTRUDE

Ysentrude, see that the sick man be not disturbed. The
Lady Elizabeth and I will sleep to-night in the great
guest chamber.

The DUCHESS *goes to* YSENTRUDE *and, leaning on
her arm, directs her towards the exit away from the closet. As
she reaches the side of the stage, she calls back to* LEWIS.

DUCHESS

My son, my son, beware of your wife's witchery.
Likely she has the witchcraft.

Exeunt the DUCHESS *and* YSENTRUDE. ELIZA-
BETH *looks frightened and clings to* LEWIS'S *arm.*

ELIZABETH *as though excusing her mother-in-law*
Thy lady mother is much provoked by me. Yesterday
she chid me for my custom of sitting by thee at meals
and said that this time of thy return I must sit seemly
with my gentlewomen. The scandal given by my sitting beside thee—up amongst the men—could scarcely
be greater wert thou not my liege and husband.

LEWIS

Yet Monk Robert once before told her not to mind
this breach of custom. He said that since we love each
other beyond what can be believed, we therefore seek
every occasion of being together.

ELIZABETH

The Duchess does not know that Master Conrad has

forbidden me to eat foods wrongly gotten or impress-
ed of the poor, nor does she know that by thy smiles or
sighs I am shown what I may eat without injustice;
wine from thy vineyards and meat killed in the chase.
To-day, thank God, we fared well, I and those especial
ladies who observe, along with me, this instruction of
Master Conrad. To-morrow when I ride forth with
thee, I shall be full of strength.

LEWIS

Thou art hardy as my hawk, or as the mare Farizer,
with her broad breast, and her wide hooves that make
sure her going. Thou art hard and clean as the steel of
my sword. But hast thou greatly tired thyself since I
left thee?

ELIZABETH

Thou who never eatest food flavoured, nor drinkest
ale, denying thyself that the body be in discipline, thou
knowest well that the body must be tamed. The fight
is stiff; the body would sleep, the soul would pray; the
body would ease her, the soul would have her fare
forth to ease some other body; so it goes, dear brother.

LEWIS

Well, in spite of all thou art ever gay, not like the scare-
devils of this court who measure their piety by the
length of their faces. They act as scare-God rather than
as scare-devil.

ELIZABETH laughs.

I will go now to see our babes. I will return shortly, for

gone all the yesterdays.
Summer gone, and daylight;
for thou —soon gone—
thou dearer than myself.

O Lewis, Lewis, Lewis,
I never thought to love the cross so little!
Felon looking on gibbet
reared up to break his bones
must feel as I—
all emptied—terrified.
O cross, and did Christ raise you
from sign of infamy to sign of triumph?
I feel this cross—taken in cruel secret—
as being my gallows, breaking me to death.

LEWIS
Should I then refuse
the garnish of this sign?
Hang back when others take Jerusalem?
When men made mock of thee I did defend thee,
and shall I stand aside while Saracen
spits on the tomb of Christ?

ELIZABETH
Were I all spirit
centred quite in soul,
my highest part the only part of me,
I'd smile and say: "Brother, be gone."
But I am flesh and blood, quite filled with passion
and all my woman being cries aloud:
"Oh, stay and leave me not!"
e

Could I but go with thee and ride beside thee
I'd clap my hands
sing: "Juche: Jubilo."
But I am weighted with the child begotten,
I should impede thy way.

LEWIS
Did I ever say:
"Love not thy Lord so well?"
Now of thy love for me
wilt build up wall
to out-screen God?

ELIZABETH
Oh, rest me in thine arms,

Clambering on to his knee

Replant me in my native soil.
I am uprooted plant;
my every fibre
is bleeding from the cut of iron spade.
Let me draw strength
from thee, heroic.

LEWIS
And have I ever pinioned thee,
or bound thee to my wrist, or hooded thee?
I never grudged
though many nights
didst leave my side
to kneel upon the floor

and turn thy heart
all towards the heavenly lover of thy soul.
I did not sleep. I felt upon my hand
thy many tears; I knew them for a balm
which flowed from thee, my loved Elizabeth,
to sweet the soil, to sweet the very air,
of sin-infected realms.
I gave thee Master Conrad for confessor,
he chastened thee with rod and wrath and fast;
I did not save thee.
I know the circuit of our steep ascent
goes hard towards perfection.
I let thee mount unhampered, so let me.
Help me to leave thee, bless me as I go,
only the lode-star of our Saviour's tomb
could draw me from the sweetness of thy breast.

ELIZABETH
Be silent, whilst I listen to thy heart.
Its steady pulse, its minstrel measure,
shall teach me say the word it seems to rhyme.
❧ *She listens to his heart.* ❧
Jesus! Jesus! Jesus! So is its beat.

❧ ELIZABETH *slips off her husband's knee, holds the
crusader's cross in one hand and his hand in her other.* ❧

This must be borne—
this can be borne, and shall be.
Belovèd will of God
I thee embrace.
Belovèd will of Lewis knit to God

I do embrace thee.
In the higher part
I am resigned.
I do embrace the cross.
❧ She kisses the crusader's cross. ❧
Christ knew its dreadful shape—
fit that the wood should rack me.

❧ Darkness overcomes them and the CHORUS MYSTI-
CUS *chants staccato. ❧*

ONE SIDE
Wounded but obedient
Elizabeth is wounded—
mortally wounded.
She chose poverty
but not this destitution;
she asked to suffer—
but not this suffering.
She loved the cross
but not this cross.
Gone yesterday
for ever,
to-morrow
storm-filled, calamitous,

OTHER SIDE *❧ singing more sharply ❧*
The wood is ripe, the wood is gathered;
the pyre is made;
the fire is nearing.
Where is the sacrifice?

❧ *Sound of trumpets.* ❧

BOTH SIDES
Lewis—Elizabeth—
Elizabeth—Lewis—
Lewis—Elizabeth
to the uttermost,
to the uttermost,
to the uttermost.

ACT III

FIRST SCENE

CHARACTERS
    ELIZABETH
    LEWIS
    RUDOLPH VON VARILA
    YSENTRUDE
    GERTA
    CRUSADERS
    AN OLD CRUSADING KNIGHT
    MEN ABOUT THE CAMP
    THE CHORUS MYSTICUS

SCENE
  In a place of jagged rocks like a picture by El Greco;
heavy clouds.

TIME
  A few weeks later.

⊛ Together in one corner of the stage, as though they had just got off their horses, are R U D O L P H, the young Graf von V A R I L A, G E R T A, and Y S E N T R U D E. They look at L E W I S and E L I Z A B E T H who are standing apart at the other side of the stage. C R U S A D E R S pass from time to time across the stage and there are sounds beyond them as of a host. If it is more pleasing to the eye, an odd hound or boy can fling down as though on the grass, for they are in the open. ⊛

RUDOLPH
Will they never finish taking leave of one another?

YSENTRUDE
Monk Robert said always that they love one another beyond what can be believed.

GERTA
All to-day the Lady Elizabeth spoke hardly at all; sighs the outcome of her heart. Instead of words, came tears.

RUDOLPH
Yesterday I heard her say: "I cannot leave thee, I cannot leave thee, I must ride with thee to the very marge of the sea."

YSENTRUDE
I heard her moan—then moan again—and at last she said: "Thy hound will follow thee into hostile land, thy horse will bear thee thither, but I shall return to shelter behind castle walls."

RUDOLPH *to* GERTA
How comes it that the Lady Elizabeth did not take leave of the Duke when his mother and his children bade him adieu?

GERTA
On the night of his going he, and those of his great faithful host, saw played the Passion of our Lord. This was done that the hearts of the host be quickened. The Count himself is captain of all this following, and of his bounty is the heavy cost of the going to Jerusalem. After the play the Duchess Sophie, the Lady Agnes, and the children of Count Lewis made their farewells to him. But Lady Elizabeth would not take her leave along with the rest: "I will go with you to the outer bounds of your dominion," she said.

GERTA moves towards LEWIS *and* ELIZABETH, *shading her eyes with her hand to look at them.*

YSENTRUDE
The children clamoured asking him to bring back a feather bird-fallen on to the holy earth of Judea; or a flower gathered. "There must be fields full of lilies," they said; and then: "Adieu, Adieu, golden Papa." And they wept, even as many hundreds of fathers and children wept together on the field.

Sound of laughter and snatches of song. A crusader or two pass along, talking and laughing.

Already the men are comforted.

RUDOLPH
All go jocund to Jerusalem; there is no other way in which to near Jerusalem.

❧ Men come on to the stage with faggots, as though to prepare a camp fire. ❧

YSENTRUDE
Were it not for the babe unborn, our Lady Elizabeth would go all the way riding, and sailing and cleaving close to her love, in heat or dust or in shower of arrows. She rode beside him often as he travelled to his people to amend the laws; often she rode with him to his hunting.

❧ An old CRUSADING KNIGHT *has joined them and listened to their conversation. ❧*

KNIGHT
Going to Palestine is no light task. In our mountains, long before we reached the sea, we once came upon a fog so heavy that we thrust against it as though it were a closed door and we, blind men, groping for exit.

Then we reached the sea. It was as the mouth of a giant death. Throaty gullets of water in which our vessel tossed, and the waves, devouring jaws, set with tusky rocks and full of foam.

In Palestine I have seen men wring out their garments to drink their sweat; they have bled their horses to drink the blood; they have drunk of even worse than

that. Other time I saw them so pressed with hunger that
they ate their own dead, so pressed that they ate the re-
surrection bodies of their christian comrades.

YSENTRUDE and GERTA cling together.

YSENTRUDE and GERTA *together*
Tell us no more! Tell us no more!

RUDOLPH
The day grows towards night, we have still a march to
do. Alas that I must part those two *designating*
ELIZABETH *and* LEWIS.

GERTA
Those two, than which no better pair ever was seen.

*RUDOLPH VON VARILA nears ELIZABETH
and LEWIS.*

RUDOLPH *to* LEWIS
Sire, let our honoured lady go, for it must be so.

*LEWIS and ELIZABETH break into tears, hold each
other clasped, and kiss each other. There is shrill of fife,
skirl of pipe, blare of trumpet; horses champing; then singing.*

RUDOLPH *to himself*
Such fanfare and tumult of faithful company, such
champing of horses, such blare of trumpet, shrill of fife,
and skirl of pipe, make it hard for a voice to be heard.

He moves back towards YSENTRUDE *and* GERTA.

YSENTRUDE
How amorous, how dolorous those two. It seems that
they cannot be parted.

*ELIZABETH, in great sorrow, wrings her hands and
speaks to* LEWIS.

ELIZABETH
Lewis, thou art become a man of steel;
familiar body prisoned in iron mesh,
caressing, hands now gloved to kill.
Oh! cursèd ore, begetter of war and wounds!
My darling, flesh no more, but turned to thing of steel.

LEWIS *to* ELIZABETH.
Elizabeth, Elizabeth, my heart's love.
Listen, my Elizabeth, my little one.
Ring with stone of sapphire will be sent as token if I
   perish in this venture.
May the Lord Christ hallow thee, and the infant, which
   thou dost carry beneath thy heart.
Hold in thy thoughts ever the remembrance of our
   life together.
And of our happy tender love.
Unitativa—benevolentia—
these the two wings of our loving,
unitativa—benevolentia—
the two eyes that have lit our loving.
And never omit my name in any one of thy prayers.

❧ ELIZABETH says nothing. She wrings her hands and moans. ❧

LEWIS
The very faithful Christ shield thy soul from scathe and guard thy courage. *❧ He moves back. ❧*

ELIZABETH
My belovèd, my belovèd. If thou returnest to me sightless, then will I be thine eyes; if maimed, then will I be thy hands and thy feet; and I will keep thy spirit in joy.

❧ YSENTRUDE runs forwards as ELIZABETH leans back into her arms. ❧

LEWIS *❧ calling from a point unseen, as though from horseback ❧* I cannot stay—Adieu—I cannot stay.

❧ The OLD CRUSADER and RUDOLPH go after LEWIS. The OLD CRUSADER comes back to look at ELIZABETH. ❧

CRUSADER *❧ to GERTA ❧*
There rides a good warrior. No sooner lady behind him than he gathered up the reins, reined in his grief, and became one with those whom he captained. Jubilant they moved forward; no other manner befits the nearing of Jerusalem although—God knows—they are yet far from the bourne. *❧ He listens. ❧*

❧ Now is heard music and the host moving away singing the song of Erzo. ❧

CRUSADER
Ah! They are singing the seafaring song of Erzo.

❧ Moving away is heard this eleventh-century song, to an air of that same century. ❧

Blessed cross
fairest tree
branches bearing
holy Burden.
Bearing blessed fruit and wholesome,
cross of Christ:
this world a sea,
God steers us,
works are the ropes,
faith is the ship,
the Holy Ghost the wind
leading us rightly.
Heaven the harbour
which we shall make;
thanks then be to God.

❧ The WOMEN *have arranged themselves in a monumental group and they listen to the music. The* OLD CRUSADER *and a few men guard them. Gloom blots them out. ❧*

ACT III

SECOND SCENE

CHARACTERS
ELIZABETH
THE DOWAGER DUCHESS

SCENE
A room on a balcony; steps lead down and across the lower stage.

TIME
Some months later.

On the rise of the curtain ELIZABETH *is resting on a bed in a high alcove. She is singing to her babe.*

ELIZABETH *singing*
Croon a rune of sweetness
to a wordless babe,
feed and rest
on my breast,
do not cry,
          rock-a-bye.

Sing a song of loving
to a baby born
fruit of love,
God above, and we two—
          cause of you.

Lord and Word: Sum of Life
keep my wordless babe
very still
in thy will.
Happy live; happy die;
rock-a-bye, rock-a-bye.

Enter SOPHIE, DOWAGER DUCHESS OF THURINGIA.

DUCHESS
I have ill tidings.

ELIZABETH
Of whom the tidings?

DUCHESS
Of Lewis.

ELIZABETH
There can be no ill come from Lewis.

DUCHESS
Yet you will sorrow.

ELIZABETH
Is he detained?

DUCHESS
He will come no more.

ELIZABETH
Then will I go to him to Jerusalem. And we will pitch a
tent near the Tomb of the Lord.

DUCHESS
Lewis is where you cannot join him: he is with angels.

ELIZABETH
Lewis is ever with angels. Yet never do the angels sun-
der but draw us closer together.

DUCHESS
Here is the ring of Lewis, and now must you understand.

☙ ELIZABETH *takes the ring and looks at it with reluc-
tance. She speaks as though she were drugged.* ❧
f

ELIZABETH
Blue stone, I know you not.
Hostile to me
as to the day the azure pall of night.
Owl-ridden, wolf-disturbed.

Stone—blue as sea—
blue, barren, watery seas that mock at thirst;
seas adverse to the earth
as you, cruel stone, to me.
Most hateful azure
blue as famine's blight.

Blue stone—strange horrid stone—
I know you not.
Nor ever saw you.
Yet a like blue
shines in the winter lightning.

She slips the ring on her finger and puts the child again to her breast. Then, suddenly, she pulls the ring off and lets the baby slip from her. Sitting bolt upright, she speaks.

O Sapphire, hardest stone,
I know you not!
And yet—and yet—
someone I loved, once said:
"This hyacinth stone
will come to show my death."
O stone, I know you!
And in this recognition
the milk within my breast is petrified.

And jewel's every part
thuds on my shuddering flesh.
So am I stoned, by sapphire stone, to death.

She rises from the bed, leaves the babe, runs through the room down the stairs and along a corridor. Flinging herself against the outermost wall, she remains huddled beneath a sheath hung on the wall, wringing her hands and crying out,
He is dead. He is dead. He is dead.

The scene is blotted out in darkness.

CHORUS MYSTICUS

ONE SIDE
Elizabeth is desolate.

OTHER SIDE
She is stricken.

ONE SIDE
Pierced by the horn of the unicorn.

OTHER SIDE
Threatened by the power of the dog.

BOTH SIDES
Tears and gall. Elizabeth is desolate; wrapped in darkness and pierced by the unicorn.

After or before the CHORUS *a sound of keening is made with bows on violins.*

ACT III

THIRD SCENE

CHARACTERS
  ELIZABETH
  GERTA
  YSENTRUDE
  ELIZABETH'S CHILDREN
  THE TWO KNIGHTS *who were seen in the court
    when the* EMPEROR *came and who will be seen
    again before the cathedral.*
  THE CHORUS MYSTICUS

SCENE
  A bare room, with grey stone walls.

TIME
  Some months later.

On the rise of the curtain THE TWO KNIGHTS, GERTA, *and* YSENTRUDE *are on the stage. The two ladies are nursing the young children and the knights sit close. They are all arranged in the centre of the stage, like a sculptured group.*

FIRST KNIGHT
I do not yet understand why we find you so ill-lodged.

YSENTRUDE
The brother of Count Lewis, the cruel Duke Henry, ordered that the Lady Elizabeth should be driven from the Castle.

GERTA
Down the steep hill we came into this Eisenach. We carried the four children, and their mother scarcely dared to look upon their pinched faces.

YSENTRUDE
In vain we knocked at doors that often enough had turned upon their hinges to let in her bounty.

GERTA
An innkeeper, kinder than the rest of the people, gave us shelter no longer needed of the swine.

YSENTRUDE
Afterwards a clerk in orders sheltered us but we were ashamed to add to his daily poverty.

GERTA
Lady Elizabeth asked the Friars Minor to sing a Te

Deum because she was glad to know the bite of poverty.

SECOND KNIGHT
Were we not to see you thus established in grief we
should hardly have accepted report of such happenings.

GERTA
The rich and the poor equally failed the Lady in her
need. For herself she heeded the cold and hunger hardly
at all but was nearly distracted to see the poor babes
suffering.

YSENTRUDE
This plight caused her to sin for she loves these children
even to excess. Their cries made her rebel against such
pitiless happenings. Often she moaned: "Out of my
love for my children should I build a wall to out-screen
God?"

GERTA
Let me sing you the ballad I have made to show the gayness and the grace of our Lady Elizabeth.

SECOND KNIGHT
Yes—sing it to us.

GERTA takes up a lute and sings.

GERTA *singing*
Through Eisenach
runs River Coriarorum
where work the tanners and the dyers.

She, ever before in litter carried
knew not how to balance
on the uneven stepping-stones.
She spread out her hands to balance
but foot slipped.
Just then an old woman
that the Lady Elizabeth
often had tended,
came now towards the Lady
and, seeing her slipping,
pushed her off the uneven stones
into the mire
fouled by the tanners and dyers.
"You would not live
like Duchess when you might have;
now that you are poor,
sink into the mud."
The Lady Elizabeth
struggled out; said, laughing:
"This as against
the jewels and the silks that I wore."
Then humbly washed her garments
in a kinder water
and returned to our hovel.

SECOND KNIGHT
We must tell the Count Varila of this for he and the
other knights will see that such wrongs be righted.
Their swords will have a say in the matter.

SECOND KNIGHT
Before the harvest they will be here, for they are bring-

ing the bones of Duke Lewis to be buried at Rheinhartsbrunn.

FIRST KNIGHT
Soon after the duke died his body was reduced to bones
whilst the knights pressed on to Jerusalem. On their return they will bring them with pomp into Allemania.

GERTA
In what manner did Count Lewis die?

FIRST KNIGHT
He called for Rudolph von Varila and for some others
and he charged us with messages and with the sapphire
ring to prove his death to Princess Elizabeth. These
things done, the Duke on deathbed, as on horseback,
faced away from all care and gathering up the reins of
mastery he went jubilant to paradise as before—jubilant
to Jerusalem. He said that the room was full of doves:
we saw a company of doves fly eastward after that he
had died.

SECOND KNIGHT
Some of us were on the sea when the news overtook
us. Very awful it was to hear the sorrowful chanting.
The lament, assurgent over wind-dented waves, was as
clang of hammer on forge of the heart—of hammer
swung by mighty arm of sorrow. *He sings.*
O heu—O heu—'las dear Lord,
brave knight how could you leave us so deserted?
Exiles on far-blown sea, on distant lands.
Light of our hearts

chief of our pilgrimage
sustainer of our courage—
woe is us . . .
O heu—O' las—O' heu O' las O'las.

One of the children cries, and they get up. GERTA *walks the child about. The* KNIGHTS *take their leave and go out.* ELIZABETH *comes in.* GERTA *puts a babe into her arms.* ELIZABETH *walks up and down with the babe.*

ELIZABETH *to* YSENTRUDE

Tell me later what the knights said. I am surfeited with grief and have ears only for the cry of the child. Let us go back to the town, to the place adjoining the inn, the place not needed of the pigs, for here the hateful looks of my hosts will frighten my babes. I have had a message that my children will be taken and cared for secretly by one who loves me. I will let them go, for they must not suffer.

She walks more quickly and speaks impetuously.
O Ysentrude, Ysentrude, how it hurts me that when I was rich I did not more for the poor. Surely the utmost reach of a woman's sufferings is to see the pale faces of her little dear creatures and to have no means of easing their hunger. I have not yet learned to reconcile my children's want with my inward peace. Nor with my resignation.

She puts the babe into YSENTRUDE'S *arms and goes to the walls of the room and strokes them.* Hearts of men, pitiless as winter! Harder than crut of oak; greedy as root of elm, root ravenous of all the nature in its soil!

Hearts of men, more pitiless than these walls. Good walls, I bless you. I thank you for the shelter that you gave us, standing between us and the wind: between us and the snow and the night. Cold walls, hard stone, warmer and more tender than the hearts of men. Good bye, I thank you for your protection. I would I could thank my hosts, but alas, I can remember nothing for which to thank them. Nevertheless, God repay them with a blessing for each one of the hurts they have done to me.

A curtain falls; it looks like a stone wall.

THE CHORUS MYSTICUS

FIRST SIDE
Tremble you that are moated in self-hood,
caparisoned in flesh,
high-turreted in pride,
and fortified in hate.

SECOND SIDE
Tremble, you of the cold hearts,
servants that should wear the livery of love,
tremble and quake;
your own frail and wretched flesh
should instruct you in pity.
Can you go unfed?
Can you go naked?

Does not your clamorous body
cry always for food, for drink, and for cover?
From the misery of your perishing flesh
can you not learn pity?
Flesh of bird and of beast stronger than yours
and more fitted to the day, to the night, and to the
    seasons.
Tremble, that you have turned away
one of God's favourites.
Now are the days of her small rains and of her naked
    furrows,
but the great powerful days of her summer
are steadily approaching.
Because of her prayer God may forgive you,
nevertheless, tremble and quake,
you of the hard hearts.

BOTH SIDES
The tears of the holy are a sweet water,
a very healing water.
They are gathered into the pitchers of God,
they are poured out to quench the fires of lust, the
    fires of anger.
They are beneficent as dew.

⚜ *Darkness falls and blots out the scene.* ⚜

ACT IV

SCENE
    Outside the Cathedral of Bamberg. If curtains alone are used for the background, they should be black. A stone seat is in the front and centre of the stage.

TIME
    About a year later.

❧ A group of about thirteen people are awaiting ELIZA-BETH *who is inside the cathedral.* ❧

RUDOLPH
The Lady Elizabeth will come to us in a little while. Whilst we await her, tell us, Ysentrude, what has happened since she sheltered here and there so miserably in the town of Eisenach. For these knights *❧ pointing❧* told us of your flight from the castle.

YSENTRUDE
Yes, we fled, our only goods what we carried in soul and heart and head.

GERTA
I learnt in that flight how poorly dowered I am in the baggage of the mind and of the soul.

YSENTRUDE
When spring came the abbess, aunt to our Lady, harboured us and the children. Later her uncle the Bishop of Bamberg here *❧ sweeping her hand towards the cathedral ❧* gave us housing and sustenance. We might have been at peace but that, alas, the bishop planned and pressed on Princess Elizabeth another marriage.

GERTA
In the lifetime of Lord Lewis she vowed to God and to her husband that were she to be widowed she would never again belong to any man.

YSENTRUDE
She trembled so at threat of re-marriage that she would

have defaced herself: "The sacrament shall not be vio-
lated by being forced on me," she said. But the wise of
the world would not believe that in truth she could be
unwilling.

GERTA
Because he who—through her uncle—pressed her
hotly to another marriage, is he that, newly widowered,
is the most powerful being in the western world.

REINHARD VON MUHLBERG
Who? Can it be that the Emperor Frederick would have
married her?

HEINRICH VON EBERSBURG
The emperor himself?

YSENTRUDE
The same. On the night when he saw the Lady Elizabeth so magnificent, so gay, he must have known
powerful liking for her.

GUNTHER VON KEFERNBURG
The lady has asked to be allowed to open the casket
that she may see the bones of her husband and take her
leave of them. This boon has been granted.

SENESCHAL HERMANN VON HOSHEIM
The more readily since she is so mistress of her regret.

RUDOLPH
Alas, alas, that I again must behold such leave-taking.

BURKHARD VON BRANDENBURG
It may be that the passing of Lewis is already of but small import to her. You saw how calm she was throughout the Mass.

HEINRICH VON EBERSBURG
One that lately saw her told me that the face of the Princess is sometimes so lit in joy that she must have forgotten her sorrow.

RUDOLPH ✿ *to* YSENTRUDE ✿
In all this buffet of misfortune how can this have been said? I, too, heard from a tattling woman of the joyful face of the Lady Elizabeth.

YSENTRUDE
The bishop, pressing the emperor's suit, said the same. I will make you the answer that I made to him. It is this: "The measure of my lady's grief is likewise the measure of her consolation." But she weeps much; and for many griefs, her own lack of faith and her demerits being cause of some of her sorrow.

RUDOLPH
But what sins has such a lady?

YSENTRUDE
No sins if you will, but often she barricades herself against grace, being over-solicitous. She does not take thought for meat or for wear; but she is anxious about this and about that; over-careful of her failings; not resting in faith. To become perfect she should be at

ease: lily of the field growing out of the breast of God; bird nesting in the branches of the Trinity.

ELIZABETH comes from the church supported by her uncle, the BISHOP. She greets the knights with tender affection and courtesy. She is clad as a poor widow; she leads her two elder children, a boy and girl aged about six and seven.

ELIZABETH
May I take seat whilst I talk with you?

The nobles spread their cloaks on the stone seat. The children stand close to her and the whole scene is tightly focussed.

Alas, that I must tell you of my griefs, but so I do and for a double purpose. First that you may move my brother Henry, through his heart out of his wrongs; wrongs done to us but more hurtful to him than ever they could be to us. I would not have him damned— the brother of Lewis. So move him through his heart . . . My further wish is that my son and my first-born girl should be given what is theirs. This daughter Sophie *showing the children to the KNIGHTS is* betrothed to the son of the Duke of Brabant, she must not be a pauper. For other two, I have but little fear; they will be cloistered; but their just endowment should be restored. And the like to me, my dowry. For Master Conrad has laid upon me certain things to be done with what is rightfully mine and until my husband's debts be paid he will not allow me to embrace a complete poverty.

g

BISHOP

Since it so much grieves her and is against her vow, I will no longer seek to wed the Duchess Elizabeth; but indeed she must be reinstated and the cause of the children must be maintained.

The KNIGHTS *talk together excitedly, one going to another and each in turn to* VON VARILA. *Then they stand in a ring round* ELIZABETH *and speak loudly.*

KNIGHTS *together*

By these swords we shall demand that Princess Elizabeth be restored and be maintained.

ELIZABETH

Sirs, say not so. I could not see bloodshed nor have my babes the cause of other children fatherless, neither shall women be unhusbanded that I be dowered. O Friends, that never. Greed of gold and greed of power, those the dreadful racks on which we stretch one another!

In years gone by, my mother murdered; yesterday, my babes driven about like leaves before wind in winter; and all for greed. There must be no battle. It were better that these children, and I, lay dead in the kind earth. Remember that I charged you to rid my brother Henry of horrid sin. That you cannot do with the sword. New from the Holy Land, can you not find some argument to melt his heart? Fresh from the tomb of Christ, can you not shoot an arrow of shame into his unthinking mind? He counts me mad and prodigal; and I would never be guardian of this dominion. I do but ask the dower I brought from Hungary; and for my children their endowments; for Henry, change of heart. Swear that you will not fight but will bring this about by power of Christ.

✧ RUDOLPH VON VARILA leading them, they swear to her on their swords to do all peacefully. ✧

Before you go forward to Rheinhartsbrunn, I will take leave of him in whom I had my joy. *✧ She gets up and moves towards the cathedral in the background. The casket is brought towards her and opened. She stoops down and passionately kisses the bones.✧*

ELIZABETH *✧ standing forward ✧*
He is dead
he is dead
he is dead.
We were one flesh—
Lewis is flesh no more.
And, in the smart of that so wounding thought
now flesh of mine
I die to you.
O winter destitution
O desolation of these whited bones!
The traffic of the blood,
the beating heart,
the illumined eye,
the outspring that was Lewis
laid silent cold and bare.
Dear bones—
image of winter's desert.

He is dead
he is dead
he is dead.
Voided of time, filled with eternity.
Now I'll deny
time and the era.
I will have no part
nor cheated be
by this sad trick of time.
He is dead
he is dead
he is dead.
He has no tie to earth;
I'll cut my ties;
will all away, my flesh, my blood, my senses,
whittle them down to fundamental bone,
do for myself what, in a shorter space,
death did for Lewis.
O God, you know how I have loved my husband;
his so delighting happy company
the only pleasure that I clamped me to.
I, who have begged in winter, know that we
merry had begged our bread through width of earth
God for our company, and each the other:
gayness and bliss.
He is dead
he is dead
he is dead.
His death love's token
laid, Christ, at thy sweet tomb.
I abandon Lewis to the will of God,
I abandon me now also to that will.

✥ She pauses. ✥
If single hair of my defeated head
could purchase back the darling of my heart,
even that petty price I would not pay
were it against God's will.
But he is dead, dead, dead.

*✥ A gradual darkness has enveloped her and now blots out
the whole scene. ✥*

CHORUS MYSTICUS

FIRST SIDE

In that sharp cry dies most her mortal part,
and in this fearful rending of her heart
the earthly part uptorn.
Her lot is cast into the realm of spirit.

SECOND SIDE

O tempest, O havoc, down-sweeping, up-rooting,
the void of this losing, O God do thou fill it.
May her sorrow be measure of thy consolation.
Consolation down-pouring—the Dove's wings o'er-
    stooping.
Dove's breast over-brooding, God's love over-bowing.

BOTH SIDES

For sorrow be comfort
come douce consolation—
consolation—consolation—
most douce consolation.

DARKNESS

ACT V

FIRST SCENE

CHARACTERS
  ELIZABETH
  YSENTRUDE
  GERTA
  A RICH WOMAN
  MASTER CONRAD
  A CROWD (*voices off*)
  THE CHORUS MYSTICUS

SCENE
  Curtains like evening, sunset with clouds; later, a bonfire.

TIME
  Two years later.

✿ Seated, focussed in the centre of the stage, are GERTA, YSENTRUDE, *and a* RICH WOMAN. MASTER CONRAD *is talking to* GERTA *and* YSENTRUDE. *✿*

MASTER CONRAD

There is no more to be said, Gerta and Ysentrude. I tell you again that in three days from now you will leave the Lady Elizabeth; and she must see you no more.

GERTA *✿ to the* RICH WOMAN *✿*

We are hounded from her, but we will not tell her of this thing until to-morrow. To-day is festal day for Elizabeth; she has summoned a multitude of people that she may share out the bounty she lately received from Hungary. Master Conrad sanctioned this giving.

RICH WOMAN

I saw in the valley a crowd seated. The Princess moved along the lines, stooped to each person.

YSENTRUDE

Many have come to watch others receiving money. I shall ever remember Elizabeth moving among the crowd, shining in her patched clothes; somehow so shining.

GERTA

Like the stars that foretold her, like the fountain where she prays.

YSENTRUDE

In a dream I heard an angel say that God sees Elizabeth

like to the moon. Alas and alas, good Master Conrad, why do you divide us? Surely Elizabeth has given up all things even to her children. Why must we too be taken from her?

MASTER CONRAD
I do not explain my decrees but I tell you this, that two peasant women will replace you. They will be my servants and they will tell me when she disobeys my commands.

RICH WOMAN
How can one so holy and so humble have disobeyed you?

MASTER CONRAD
I said to her: "Give to each of the poor but a penny a day;" and for a while she obeyed. But the clamour of the poor overcame her and then she minted silver pennies.

RICH WOMAN *laughing*
Silver pennies minted! That was well contrived!

YSENTRUDE shows the RICH WOMAN such a penny.

MASTER CONRAD
She was flogged for her wilfulness.

YSENTRUDE
Yet she was not disobedient. I see her obedience as

though it were her feet with which she runs and races to God. But the wings of her charity outspeed the feet of her obedience, and when shaft of pity pierces the heart of Elizabeth her wings are outspread—flying, flying to the need of the miserable.

GERTA

The letter of Master Conrad's order was followed, but its spirit was quite outflown. Therefore he ordered his servants to beat Elizabeth.

YSENTRUDE ✿ *to the* RICH WOMAN ✿

Then Elizabeth was gathered suddenly unto the fifth heaven.

GERTA

But when the servants told Master Conrad he said: "Next time beat her into the seventh heaven."

RICH WOMAN

Master! You are as harsh to her as to the heretics whom you chasten.

GERTA

Master Conrad says to Elizabeth: "Do not be singular." He says that to her who is single in loveliness: "Do not be singular, be prudent." As well might he say to the lone star: "Be one of many."

MASTER CONRAD

I will not have her become a pauper for the poor. I will not have her tend lepers, nor have her again mothering the leprous child that I have taken from her.

GERTA
Nor will Master Conrad allow her to withdraw from
all active works; he will not allow her to live in silence,
alone, as she entreated to do; even when she stripped
herself of her children he said: "Remain in the world;
accept the monies of Marburg; pay your husband's
debts; give bounty with prudence."

MASTER CONRAD
She is of inflexible will. I will break that will—it is nearly broken.

GERTA
You wound her in every joint, in every fibre; and she
fears you as partridge fears hawk.

MASTER CONRAD
I will take my leave of you; you will need to make pre-
paration for your departure.

CONRAD bows to them and goes out.

YSENTRUDE
It is only of late that Master Conrad has sought to cir-
cumscribe the lady in her charity. He fears that she may
beggar herself and, too, he seems bent on breaking her
will.

GERTA
He parts and sunders us from her, alas and alas. *She*

gets up and goes to a statue of Our Lady which is hung in a corner at the right-hand of the stage. She lights a candle before it. ❧ Holy Mary, Mother of God, pray for us sinners now and at the hour of our death. ❧ *She strikes her bosom and speaks as though she had understood a dreadful new thing.* ❧ But now *is* the hour of my death, for Elizabeth was my good; therefore was she my living.
Death will invade mine eyes for the light of them will be gone.
Death will be laid within the fold of my ears in a slow, a creeping grossness.
For I shall no longer hear the good words.
The silence of death will be laid upon my tongue; for I shall not give praise.
Death—in the failing of the heart—in the slow chilling of the blood.
Death in the rigor of my spirit.
Pray for me now, in this the first hour of my dying.
Now and henceforward.
Pray for me *now*, for this *now* is the hour of my death.

❧ YSENTRUDE *looks through the curtains, and bonfires burst into flame.* ❧

YSENTRUDE
See, they are lighting the good fires, the fires of joy for the comfort of those who are too old or too young to go back to-night with the crowd that Elizabeth has enriched. Do you hear?

❧ *Singing begins. The three women listen to a thread of music which comes from the direction of the fires.* ELIZA-

BETH, *barefooted and in the white habit of the third Order of Franciscans, comes in quickly. Her clothes are patched. Looking out towards the bonfires, she speaks with much animation to the women.*

ELIZABETH
O happy day, O happy, happy day ... the long rows of the people ... the lit eyes, the glad uplifted hands, lips giving blessings like honeycups of flowers full of sweetness.
O happy, happy day ... Listen how the people praise God.

They listen to music. Pulling YSENTRUDE *by the hand*

Come with me—let us join them by the open fires.
I delight to see them joyful! Listen! How good it makes men to be happy. *She pauses.* I knew always that it is good for men to be happy. We should oftener give them happiness.

CROWD *singing, off*
Thanks be to God
for wood and fire;
for young desire;
for belly's mirth;
for seed in earth,
and seed in womb,
for milk in breast;
for rest in tomb.

Thanks be to God
for love in life;
for ease, and strife;
for children's ways,
and poet's lays;
for craft of hand;
for fields, for flowers;
for hours God-planned,
thanks be to God,
thanks be to God.

❧ *Darkness falls.* ❧

ACT V

SECOND SCENE

CHARACTERS
ELIZABETH
A FRIAR OF FRANCIS
THE CHORUS MYSTICUS

SCENE
By the River Lahn.

TIME
About a year later.

✒ ELIZABETH is praying by a fountain near the River Lahn.✒

THE CHORUS MYSTICUS

FIRST SIDE

Would we could sing with song of leaping water,
with voice of fountain by the which she prays,
or sound of placid Lahn, pellucid river.
Linked to Elizabeth these things of silver,
the sheen of moon and water in her ways.

SECOND SIDE

We would instruct how that she mars her days,
being solicitous, though not for bread;
nor is she troubled as from whence her clothing;
but fails in perfectness—as ever needing
assurance that the love of God is shed
about her, mantling her.

FIRST SIDE

                     Her will is wed
to will of God. But she should encompass rest
like bird of air enfolded in the nest;
like lily of the field serene in sod.
Quiètly growing out of hand of God,
and should be nested in the Trinity—
the spreading branches of the Trinity.
For how should creature than Creator be
more loving and more giving?
Nor could it be that Love should be out-loved.

ELIZABETH

Mary Magdalen, by the merit of your tears, loosen my tears. *☙ She stretches her hands towards the fountain.☙* Fountain I watch you, but my soul is no longer like to you; you spring upwards, I am tied to earth; you are gay and clean and shining—I am sad and sullied; unto you—Water —parched and thirsting I come. *☙ She wrings her hands.☙*

Africa in my soul.
In torrid zone, on equatorial line,
I stand unsheltered
and have not
even a shadow left—
so stark alone.
Sahara-wide about me
sameness stretches.
The birds are brown;
the things that grow have thorns;
no water is—
God has forgotten me.

The sins of men,
like grains of desert sand, uncountable.
In dust-storm of their sins the hope of heaven
is vain, is mirage;
the very death of Christ made unavailing:
that death, oasis sure,
water and date-palm;
yet the travellers pass
and find it not—and perish.
h

As swarm of locust, gorged with all the green
of lands made barren,
so my sorrow, gorged.
My daily bread, the locusts of my sorrow
fired in the ashes of my resignation.
Come God—and bless
my dish of locusts—and my cup of tears.

&⊗ A FRIAR OF FRANCIS, *who was seen in Act II,
Scene I, and who was Confessor to the young* ELIZABETH
before MASTER CONRAD *was given charge of her, approaches* ELIZABETH. ⊗&

ELIZABETH
O Father, you who guided me when I was but a child,
tell me something of comfort, for God seems very far
away.

FRIAR
What is your distress? I heard that justice had been done
to you and to your children. What is it that afflicts you?

ELIZABETH
That men are so sinful and that God is far off; and, too,
I fear Master Conrad and can tell him nothing. He
comes to me smelling of the smoke of the pyres where
he has burned heretics, sooted of the smoke; and I
tremble, for I hardly dare ask myself—do I myself believe?

FRIAR
What is that you are saying?

ELIZABETH

Oh, it must be that I believe, but of late I believe without joy and without relish of conviction. I love God,
but can scarce conceive that he loves me. For how
should Light love darkness?

FRIAR

This dryness of soul comes from your hatred of sin, and
from your love of God; but you must trust him. Look,
Elizabeth. *He shows her a willow growing on the other
side of the river.* It were less miracle for that tree to
leave its bank and come over to this side than for you,
creature, to out-love God-Creator; God, Spirit of love.

A heavy wind blows.

ELIZABETH *crying out*

Look, Father, as you speak, how, in the high wind, the
willow sweeps towards us.

Blot out SCENE. CHORUS MYSTICUS *takes
up,*

BOTH SIDES

O by the merit of the ghostly water,
the sacramental, the baptismal water,
may she be rid of dryness spiritual.

ACT V

THIRD SCENE

CHARACTERS
  ELIZABETH
  RUDOLPH VON VARILA
  A CRIPPLE
  A MONK
  TWO PRIESTS
  TWO WOMEN
  THE CHORUS MYSTICUS

SCENE
  Amethyst curtains.

TIME
  A little later.

ELIZABETH and RUDOLPH VON VARILA *are sitting together. They occupy the middle of the stage.* ELIZABETH *is spinning with a wheel. She is clad in poverty.*

VARILA
Whoever saw a King's daughter spinning?

ELIZABETH
Rudolph von Varila has seen it.

VON VARILA laughs.

ELIZABETH
So, Rudolph von Varila, you come to me to warn me! I obey Master Conrad, I make journeys on his account, return at his beck and therefore some have said that he is my lover. A strange lover, Rudolph. Look. *She shows bruises on her shoulder.* VARILA *exclaims.*

I forgot something he told me, or did not understand, and so I disobeyed. He thought I was wilful.

VARILA
My lady, my lady.

ELIZABETH *She laughs a little. She gets up and reaches towards a basket for a fresh bobbin.*
And yet, Master Conrad is good to me. I fear him, but I reverence him. His ways are harsh but he does not either spare himself, and he is fearless, upbraiding the rich as often as the poor. He who could be rich lives in

austerity, he is upright and learned. Lewis and the Pope chose him to be my guide, and well has he guided me, though sometimes I lament the departure of the Friar of Francis who was with me before Master Conrad came.

VARILA

Lady, lady! As to this evil rumour, you must know that I never sullied you in thought. I told you of this rumour only that you might ward against the vile thing.

ELIZABETH picks up from the floor a big marguerite which is lying in a bunch of wild flowers.

ELIZABETH *holding the flower*

Look, Rudolph, a symbol. That wild flower is as I was, the silver petals the things belonging to me so closely they were part of myself as petal is part of flower. Now, Rudolph, one by one, the petals went. Some of them went by God's will, others went through man's malice, others again I myself have undone. Look. *She holds up the flower and pulls out petal by petal.* There goes a petal—my mother—murdered when I was a child. There the Duke Hermann, father of Lewis. He protected me from the Duchess Sophia and from the courtiers. He loved me. *She pulls out two petals.* There is one for him and one for his protection.

Then Lewis went. *She pulls out lots of petals.* His death stripped me.

Then my state, my pomp, *pulling petals at each word* my wealth, my roof when we were driven out.

Then my children, Rudolph. *She pulls out one, two, three, four.* I could not keep them. I loved them to excess. For their sake and according to God's will as I understood it—Adieu.

And Ysentrude   *a petal*

And Gerta   *another petal*

My strength   *another*

My beauty   *another*

My lepers   *another*

My poor   *another*

My works   *another*

And now, Rudolph, the last petal—the petal of my white name. *She flings it away; then gets up and wrings her hands.* Oh, may my children never hear me defamed! *She covers her face with her hands.*

VARILA

But the golden heart is as golden as ever, and you cannot be sullied. Is the purity of this river sullied if a man throw in handful of foulness?

ELIZABETH *looking happier*

Rudolph, you console me. I will tell you something I never told to any other. I am prevented now from giving money; I may not nurse lepers; I may not live alone in contemplation though that is my desire. Yet since I have been so strictly held I have gained great power in prayer. I am strangely able to help people; and souls departed I can also help.

VARILA *laughing tenderly*

O lady, I have heard of your prayers for the young sinful man and how your burning charity enveloped him in a cloak of such heat that he cried out to you to stop your prayer. I know, too, how his cold heart was melted by your ardour. He has now given himself over to the service of God—he who surely was pawn of the devil.

A CRIPPLE comes on to the stage, walking with two sticks. He need not look poor, but he is ill. He approaches ELIZABETH. She rises to greet him.

CRIPPLE
Lady Elizabeth, Lady Elizabeth I have come from the well of strange water, from the place where I have seen you pray by the tomb of your husband. I come to you that you may heal me.

ELIZABETH *shocked*
But I cannot heal you.

CRIPPLE
Princess Elizabeth, in the name of Lewis, by the virtue of your love of Lewis, I entreat you to heal me.

At the mention of Lewis's name ELIZABETH spreads out her hands, then lays them on the cripple's shoulders and she looks at him with such an intensity of love in her eyes that the CRIPPLE slowly straightens himself. VARILA goes to the cripple to support him.

Crying out
Love went out from her, like a flood, like a spate.

I am becoming straight—I am growing.
The lady's love has worked a miracle.

VARILA

By the love in her eyes when you said the name of Lewis!

CRIPPLE

I felt it strong as the sea at a spring tide, a healing warmth that lapped about me and took away my ill. Thank you, lady.

ELIZABETH

It is God you must thank. I am but as a water-reed through which can blow the harmony of God. Come and praise him. *She pulls him towards an open window.* VARILA *follows.* ALL *are blotted out in purple. Crescendo of* CHORUS MYSTICUS

FIRST SIDE

Behold the power of love.

SECOND SIDE

Behold how good is love.

FIRST SIDE

Behold the power of love.

BOTH SIDES

Behold the saints.

FIRST SIDE

They are stored with God,

they are charged with God,
they are fulfilled with God.

BOTH SIDES
They are deified.

SECOND SIDE
Virtue goes out from them;
their very garments
saturate with love.

BOTH SIDES
See how strong is love.
See how strong is love.
Behold the saints.
Behold power.
Behold love.

SCENE
   A truckle bed veiled in white in the middle of the stage.

   A few figures—MEN, MONKS, *and* TWO WOMEN
—*and the* CHORUS MYSTICUS.
Music is heard.

A WOMAN
We do not hear music, but Elizabeth seems to hear it.

SECOND WOMAN
What a strange singing it was that came from her bed.
Was it she that was singing? Her lips did not seem to
move.

A MONK
I asked her whence the sound, for to me it seemed like
the song of a bird. She told me she had sung to some—
invisible—who to her are singing.

ELIZABETH *indistinctly seen and as though talking to
herself and with threads of song coming faintly from the bed*
Tell me about water, speak to me of sweet humble
water seeking ever the lowest place.

CHORUS MYSTICUS

FIRST SIDE
God has transfixed the matter of this earth
and fired it with his love; all creatures show
the traces of the Blessed Trinity,
and linked again—as by a stronger wedlock,
for purposes of sacramental rites,
some certain things have properties divine.
So very Love is mantled in the oil
of olives crushed, and in the juice of grapes
pressed and down-trodden.
God enters in the corn—and it is God.
Wine; water; chrism; words; and oil become
the special sure conveyances of love.
And very Love wears water for a garment,
so makes a chariot of the running rills
to overtake the souls of earth-born men,
hides him in water; raises it in power
to laver souls.

ELIZABETH
Tell me now of stars, for I think of the Wise Kings and
of the star guiding—of all the good stars.

SECOND SIDE
That Christ-star was no planet nor belonged
to furniture of heaven.
Its orbit leaving
it shone in light of day.
Contrariwise took course
from north to south,
moving from Persia to Jerusalem.
It was, for sure, a power endowed with reason.
We heard a seraph say
that Christ-sign was a cloak of starry shape
the Holy Ghost did on.

*A bell is heard striking midnight. Then a cock is heard
crowing.* ELIZABETH *sits up in bed and speaks rather excitedly.*

ELIZABETH
Midnight; cockcrow; the hour when the Word was
    spoken—
When the Light shone—when Christ was born!

The cock crows again.

So crowed cock long ago, long ago,
day in azure vault, up-sprang, out-sprang;
so crowed cock far ago, far ago,
winter solstice over:

prime of the green, of the gold,
the spring-time uprising.
So crowed cock, long ago, long ago,
the Out-come of God,
out-branched, took virgin flesh;
the woman on tiptoe, up-reaching, up-tending,
answering Love with love the while God overbowed.
Sap of the earth meeting light of the sun.
The day-spring; the year-spring; the Off-Spring
    of heaven—
at cock-crow far ago, far ago—
yesterday—this day—everyday—and for ever.

ELIZABETH dies. A great sound of clapping hands. A woman says

"It is as though a company of wood-pigeons was rising from out of a forest."

The auditorium may be flooded with sweet perfume. Triumphant music is heard and the CHORUS MYSTICUS *says or chants:*

FIRST SIDE
By stars fore-shown, by voiceless night foretold;
by poets fore-hoped, by Spirit of love fore-thought,
predestined soul; prefigured darling spirit.

SECOND SIDE
Free-choosing soul—had courage failed, or love,
stars—poets—God—had failed their expectation.

FIRST SIDE
Thy circle now made perfect, and thy course
stayed at that heavenly point whence it was drawn.

SECOND SIDE
The divine Narcissus over-stooped this soul,
and saw his beauty mirrored—water-wise—
reflected in the crystal of the soul.

FIRST SIDE
And now in light of glory—water-wise
this soul will hold the vision beatific;
yet, guarded safe, the imperishable self;
the separate bliss; the everlasting I.

BOTH SIDES
Blessed the pure in heart;
blessed the crystal waters.
Elizabeth shall see God;
she shall see God.
She shall see God.

FINISHED